PARTY
PLANNER

First published in the United Kingdom in 1994 by
Ebury Press Stationery Limited
Random House UK Limited Reg. No. 954009

1 3 5 7 9 10 8 6 4 2
Copyright © Random House UK Ltd 1994

Introduction by Moyra Fraser, Good Housekeeping Magazine

Set in Horley Old Style by
SX Composing Limited, Rayleigh, Essex
Printed and bound in Hong Kong

Designed by Polly Dawes

ISBN 0 09 178316 X

Cover illustration:
Writing, 1914 (Mary Evans Picture Library)

PARTY
PLANNER

EBURY PRESS STATIONERY

INTRODUCTION

For many people organising a party, no matter how small, can be a daunting task. How do you cope? The trick is to plan it so you can enjoy the occasion too. The most difficult, and most crucial part of giving a party is sitting down, pen in hand, to work out the details. Pre-planning will always pay the highest dividends.

The aim of the Party Planner is to provide a guiding hand to help you plan well ahead and really enjoy your entertaining. It's divided into helpful sections that will enable you to keep a record of every detail of the party from the chosen menu and shopping list to the seating arrangements and table decorations.

Hints and tips for achieving a successful party are also included. You'll find advice on how to cope with cooking for large numbers, what to do if you need extra glasses and lots more, plus a useful buffet quantity chart. There's also a section at the back for keeping a note of your favourite suppliers' names and addresses.

Whether you want to have a supper party for 10 or a buffet for 200, the Party Planner will help you prepare the perfect party with the minimum of fuss.

Moyra Fraser

PLANNING THE MENU

A five-course dinner for eight, a casual supper party for friends, a drinks party with buffet or a barbecue in the garden – whichever type of party you choose, careful planning in advance will remove all the stress and enable you to enjoy yourself.

Whichever size of party you are having, planning the menu is always important.

- Choose the dishes you want to serve and list them, adding the references to cookery books and page numbers where necessary.
- Highlight any dishes on your list that will freeze successfully and can therefore be cooked in advance.
- Read through the recipes, plan when to cook each one and start to make a shopping list (this page can be torn out when you want to use it).
- Don't forget to add any garnishes and 'extras' like bread and butter, coffee, sugar and milk.

TIP

- Keep your menu simple and within your capabilities, stick to dishes that have been successful in the past rather than try something new and elaborate.

EQUIPMENT

When planning your menu think carefully how you are going to cook, store or reheat food. Do you have enough crockery and cutlery to serve all the dishes? You may need to borrow or hire extra supplies.

- Don't forget to make a shopping list of accessories like paper napkins, candles and flowers.

CHOOSING DISHES

The choice of dishes depends on a number of factors. Some of your guests may be vegetarians or on special diets. Do any of them dislike particular foods? You can make a note of these points when you are writing out your guest list.

- Try to achieve a balance of flavours, textures and colours in the food you serve.
- The "wet and dry" rule is a good one to follow; a 'wet' course, such as soup or casserole, should precede a 'dry' one, such as grilled steak or a fruit tart.
- Bear in mind how health-conscious most people are today, and avoid planning a meal with several rich courses.
- Seasonal food will always be cheapest and freshest.
- Planning your dishes will ensure that you have plenty of time to be with your guests.
- Avoid dishes that need careful timing, such as a soufflé, as this will not allow for guests who may not be punctual.

COOKING FOR LARGE NUMBERS

A buffet party is an ideal choice if you want to feed large numbers of guests. Decide on your menu well in advance because of the quantities and logistics involved (see the chart at the end of the section for advice on quantities).

- Do not just quadruple your favourite recipe – cooking times may vary significantly if the volume is increased.
- Offer a good balance of sweet and savoury dishes, choosing dishes that can be frozen well in advance like quiches, flans, pâtés, tarts, pastries, sandwich fillings, cakes and gateaux.

TIPS
- The more people you are feeding the less you need to allow per head. For 100 people 85 portions should be enough.
- Have several serving points for the buffet food and drinks, this avoids bottlenecks.
- Arrange the table so guests can progress naturally around from plates and cutlery, to main dishes and the side dishes.
- Your buffet table will be the focal point of the party so make it temptingly attractive.

FREEZING
- A microwave oven is useful for last minute reheating but always ensure that you reheat food until it is piping hot.
- Dishes suitable for freezing can be cooked well in advance. Make a note of how much thawing and final cooking time each dish needs and label packages carefully.
- After cooking, cool food for freezing as quickly as possible, then freeze immediately.

THE CHEESE BOARD

Decide for yourself or ask your guests, whether they prefer cheese immediately after the main course or as an end to the meal.

- If buying cheese in advance take into account the degree it will mature before it is served.
- Always remove cheese from the refrigerator and unwrap it at least 1 hour before serving.
- A conventional cheese board would include four cheeses; one soft, one hard or semi hard, one blue and one other, perhaps a goat's cheese.
- Serve a selection of crackers, biscuits and some rolls or French bread to accompany the cheese. Offer unsalted butter.

COFFEE

- Use freshly roasted and ground beans and freshly boiled water.
- Allow about 25 g (1 oz) coffee per 300 ml (½ pint) water.

DRINKS

What you give your guests to drink is just as important as the food.

- Pimms and other long, cool drinks, chilled white wine and fruit wine cups are ideal for summer parties.
- A warm glass of mulled wine or punch is a welcoming drink in the winter.
- Always have a good supply of non-alcoholic drinks.

TIPS

- Remember to make or buy plenty of ice in advance.
- Allow approximately ½ to ¾ bottle of wine per person.
- One bottle of wine should give 6 glasses.

WINE

It is worth keeping notes of wines, the ones which you particularly like, with what foods they were served and how well they went together.

TIPS

- Serve a light wine with light food, a full-bodied one with full flavoured dishes.
- Serve white wines before red, dry before sweet, light bodied before more full-bodied, young before old, less expensive before expensive.
- Wines of a region are the best accompaniments for the foods from the region.

General Tips

- If you need extra glasses, try your local wine merchant first, they may let you borrow them for free if you buy your party drinks from them. Check whether you can return them unwashed.
- Large candles left burning at safe points around a room will help clear smoke from the air. Ordinary candles will do or you can buy special "smokers candles".
- Leave plenty of ashtrays strategically placed around a room.

BUFFET QUANTITY CHART

Below are the approximate quantities to serve 12 people. For 25 people, multiply the quantities by two. For 50 people multiply by four. For 75 people multiply by five and a half. For 100 people multiply by seven.

Cocktails Eats
Allow about 80 small eats for 12 people to serve before a meal.
Allow about 120 small eats for 12 people to serve alone.

Starters
Soups	allow 2.6 litre (4½ pints) for 12
Pâtés	allow 1.1 kg (2½ lb) for 12
Smoked Salmon	allow 900 g (2 lb) for 12
Prawns	900 g (2 lb) for 12

Main Dishes
Boneless chicken or turkey	allow 1.8 kg (4 lb) for 12
Whole chicken	allow three 1.4 kg (3 lb) for oven ready birds for 12
Turkey	allow one 5.5 kg (12 lb) oven ready bird for 12

Lamb/beef/pork
boneless	allow 2–2.3 kg (4½–5 lb) for 12
on the bone	allow 3.2–3.6 kg (7–8 lb) for 12
mince	allow 2 kg (4½ lb) for 12

Fish
Whole with head	allow 2.3 kg (5 lb) for 12
Steaks	allow twelve 175 g (6 oz) steaks for 12
Fillets	allow 2 kg (4½ lb) for 12
Prawns	allow 1.4 kg (3 lb) for 12 (main course)

Buffet Quantity Chart

Accompaniments

Potatoes, roast and mashed	allow 2 kg (4½ lb) for 12
new	allow 1.8 kg (4 lb) for 12
Rice and pasta	allow 700 g (1½ lb) for 12
Green vegetables	allow 1.4 kg (3 lb) for 12
Fresh spinach	allow about 3.6 kg (8 lb) for 12

Salads

Tomato	allow 700 g (1½ lb) 12
Salad leaves	allow 2 medium heads for 12
Cucumber	allow 1 large for 12
French dressing	allow 175 ml (6 fl oz) for 12
Mayonnaise	allow 300 ml (10 fl oz) for 12

Bread

Fresh bread	allow 1 large loaf for 12
Medium sliced bread	allow 1 large loaf for 12 (approx 24 slices)

Cheeses

For a wine and cheese party	allow 1.4 kg (3 lb) for 12
To serve at the end of a meal	allow 700 g (1½ lb) for 12

Butter

To serve with bread or biscuits and cheese	allow 225 g (8 oz) for 12
To serve with bread and biscuits and cheese	allow 350 g (12 oz) for 12
For sandwiches	allow 175 g (6 oz) softened butter for 12 rounds

Cream

For pudding or dessert	allow 569 ml (20 fl oz) single cream for 12
For coffee	allow 300 ml (10 fl oz) single cream for 12

Milk

allow 450 ml (15 fl oz) for 12 cups tea

Coffee and Tea

Ground coffee	allow about 125 g (4 oz) for 12 medium cups
Instant	allow about 75 g (3 oz) for 12 large cups
Tea	allow about 25 g (1 oz) for 12 medium cups

DECORATIONS/ACCESSORIES

TABLE PLAN

Timetable

Day(s) Before

Evening Before

TIMETABLE

PARTY DAY A.M.

P.M.

Decorations/Accessories

Table Plan

Timetable

Day(s) Before

_____

_____

_____

_____

_____

_____

_____

Evening Before

_____

_____

_____

_____

_____

_____

_____

_____

_____

_____

TIMETABLE

PARTY DAY A.M.

P.M.

TIMETABLE

PARTY DAY A.M.

P.M.

PARTY PLANNER

OCCASION

DATE

TIME

GUESTS

MENU PLANNER

DISHES

RECIPE SOURCE

SHOPPING LIST

SHOPPING LIST

Decorations/Accessories

_____

_____

_____

_____

_____

_____

_____

_____

_____

Table Plan

TIMETABLE

DAY(S) BEFORE

EVENING BEFORE

TIMETABLE

PARTY DAY A.M.

P.M.

PARTY PLANNER

OCCASION

DATE

TIME

GUESTS

MENU PLANNER

DISHES

RECIPE SOURCE

Shopping List

Shopping List

Table Plan

Timetable

Day(s) Before

_____

_____

_____

_____

_____

_____

Evening Before

_____

_____

_____

_____

_____

_____

_____

_____

_____

TIMETABLE

PARTY DAY A.M.

P.M.

PARTY PLANNER

OCCASION

DATE

TIME

GUESTS

MENU PLANNER

DISHES

RECIPE SOURCE

SHOPPING LIST

SHOPPING LIST

Decorations/Accessories

_____

_____

_____

_____

_____

_____

_____

_____

_____

Table Plan

TIMETABLE

DAY(S) BEFORE

_____

_____

_____

_____

_____

_____

EVENING BEFORE

_____

_____

_____

_____

_____

_____

_____

_____

_____

_____

TIMETABLE

PARTY DAY A.M.

P.M.

PARTY PLANNER

OCCASION

DATE

TIME

GUESTS

Menu Planner

DISHES

RECIPE SOURCE

SHOPPING LIST

SHOPPING LIST

Decorations/Accessories

_____

_____

_____

_____

_____

_____

_____

_____

_____

Table Plan

TIMETABLE

DAY(S) BEFORE

EVENING BEFORE

TIMETABLE

PARTY DAY A.M.

P.M.

PARTY PLANNER

OCCASION

DATE

TIME

GUESTS

MENU PLANNER

DISHES

RECIPE SOURCE

SHOPPING LIST

Shopping List

Decorations/Accessories

_____

_____

_____

_____

_____

_____

_____

_____

_____

_____

Table Plan

TIMETABLE

DAY(S) BEFORE

EVENING BEFORE

Timetable

PARTY DAY A.M.

P.M.

PARTY PLANNER

OCCASION _____

DATE _____

TIME _____

GUESTS _____

DISHES

RECIPE SOURCE

SHOPPING LIST

SHOPPING LIST

Decorations/Accessories

Table Plan

TIMETABLE

DAY(S) BEFORE

EVENING BEFORE

Timetable

PARTY DAY A.M.

P.M.

SPECIALIST SUPPLIERS

NAME

ADDRESS

TELEPHONE

NAME

ADDRESS

TELEPHONE

NAME

ADDRESS

TELEPHONE

NAME

ADDRESS

TELEPHONE

NAME

ADDRESS

TELEPHONE

SPECIALIST SUPPLIERS

NAME

ADDRESS

TELEPHONE

NAME

ADDRESS

TELEPHONE

NAME

ADDRESS

TELEPHONE

NAME

ADDRESS

TELEPHONE

NAME

ADDRESS

TELEPHONE

SPECIALIST SUPPLIERS

NAME

ADDRESS

TELEPHONE

NAME

ADDRESS

TELEPHONE

NAME

ADDRESS

TELEPHONE

NAME

ADDRESS

TELEPHONE

NAME

ADDRESS

TELEPHONE

SPECIALIST SUPPLIERS

NAME

ADDRESS

TELEPHONE

NAME

ADDRESS

TELEPHONE

NAME

ADDRESS

TELEPHONE

NAME

ADDRESS

TELEPHONE

NAME

ADDRESS

TELEPHONE